NINJA KID 5

NINJA CLONES!

Scholastic Press
An imprint of Scholastic Australia Pty Limited (ABN 11 000 614 577)
PO Box 579 Gosford NSW 2250
www.scholastic.com.au

Part of the Scholastic Group
Sydney • Auckland • New York • Toronto • London • Mexico City • New Delhi • Hong Kong • Buenos Aires • Puerto Rico

First published by Scholastic Australia in 2020.

A catalogue record for this book is available from the National Library of Australia

Typeset in Bizzle-Chizzle, featuring Hola Bisou and Handblock.

ISBN 978-93-5471-972-1

This reprint edition: January 2026

Printed in India at MicroPrints India, New Delhi

ANH DO

illustrated by Anton Emdin

NINJA KID 5

NINJA CLONES!

A Scholastic Press book
from Scholastic Australia

ONE

My name is **Nelson Kane.** For most of my life, I was just a normal kid. Well, a normal, nerdy kid.

But when I woke up on my tenth birthday, I had become

NiNJA KiD!

But I'm still a huge

NERD.

My ninja powers came from my **dad**, who **went missing** many years ago.

I live in a **junkyard** in **Duck Creek** with my **mum**, my **grandma** and my **cousin Kenny**.

When I'm **NINJA KID**, Kenny is my **awesome sidekick, H-DUDE!**

Kenny is funny, loyal and ALWAYS hungry.

Grandma is one of the world's greatest inventors. But her inventions sometimes take a while to get right! Like the mechanical mosquito-eating plant she created. It bites off way more than it can **chew!**

Or there's the bed that makes itself...

just not always when you want it to!

Duck Creek used to be a **peaceful** town . . .

but lately, things have been really

CRAZY!

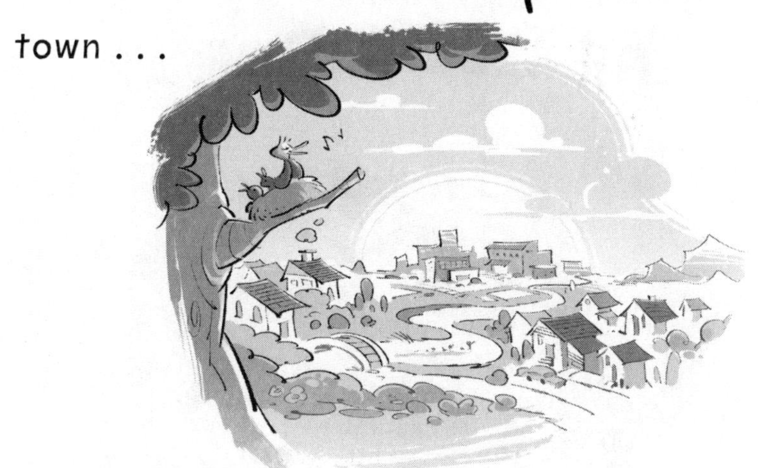

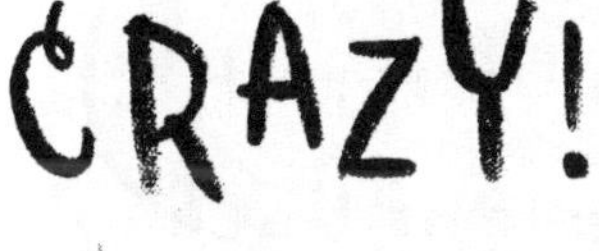

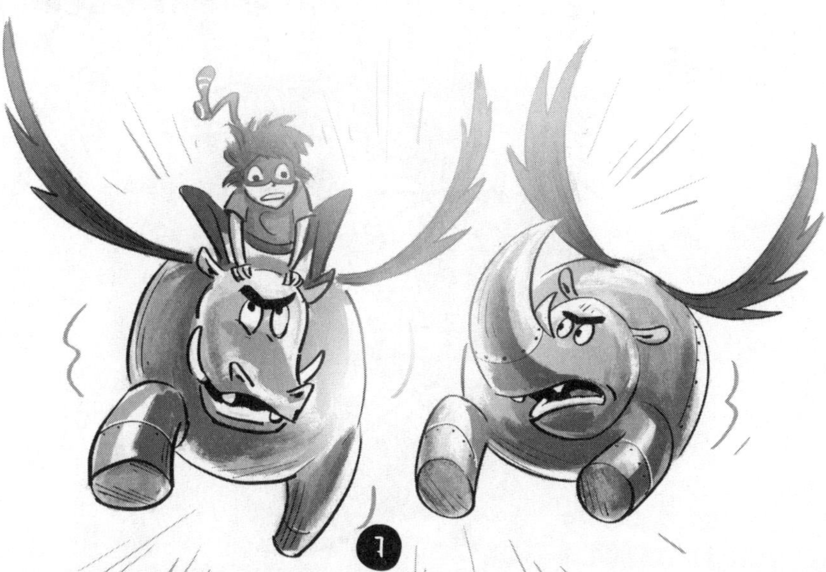

And it's all because of one man . . .

DR ANDREW KANE.

Dr Kane is my dad's **twin** brother. He is trying to drive everyone out of **Duck Creek.**

He's come up with all sorts of **nasty** plans to help him achieve his goal . . .

Last time he was in Duck Creek, he invaded the **CIRCUS!** He had giant robot animals with him to scare everyone out of town . . .

And a crazy new sidekick - **EINSTEIN THE CHIPMUNK!**

Luckily, Kenny and I have managed to stop Dr Kane each time, without giving away our **identities**.

Even though Dr Kane has gone for now, we know he won't give up. He'll be back.

But today we've got a bigger problem . . .

a maths test!

Kenny and I stayed up way **too late** studying. At least, that was the plan.

But it was hard to study when I kept getting distracted by a `really cool lasso` Grandma made for me. It had a special GPS tracker built in, so it was nearly impossible to miss!

And Kenny had an **EPIC** eating competition . . .

with himself!

So when our alarm went off in the morning, **we slept right through it.**

Luckily, Grandma invented **another** alarm clock that **REALLY** wakes you up when you sleep in!

'We didn't get nearly enough sleep,' I said to Kenny with a giant yawn. 'We went to sleep at **two o'clock** in the morning. Now we're up at **seven o'clock!'**

'What's the problem?' said Kenny. 'That's TEN HOURS of sleep. We'll smash this maths test!'

TWO

I was so **tired** that when we walked into the kitchen, I thought I was seeing things. Sitting next to Mum and Grandma were . . . us?!

WHAT THE?!

Kenny was so **sleepy** he didn't even notice something was out of the ordinary! 'Hi, Grandma. Hi, Aunty. Hi, Kenny and Nelson,' he said.

Was I dreaming? I rubbed my eyes and looked again. They were still there, smiling back at me.

'Ahhh . . . what's going on?' I asked.

'Nelson and Kenny, meet your **ROBOT CLONES!**' Grandma said.

It was **INCREDIBLE.** The clones looked EXACTLY like us. Even Mum had trouble telling my clone and me apart!

'Finally someone who understands what it's like to be me!' Kenny said.

'Why did you make **clones** of us, Grandma?' I asked.

'That's obvious,' Kenny said. 'Because we're **AWESOME!**'

'You are awesome, but that's not quite the reason,' Grandma said.

'Some of your **friends** have noticed you both go **missing** whenever Ninja Kid and H-Dude are around,' Mum explained.

'And if your friends are getting **suspicious**, then Dr Kane definitely would be, too,' Grandma said.

'Grandma created these clones so that the next time Ninja Kid and H-Dude are needed, your clones can make it look like you're still there,' Mum said.

'**Super cool** idea!' I said.

'And our clones can do more than just stand in for us,' Kenny said. 'They can do all the things we hate doing! Cleaning, dishes, homework . . .'

'No,' Grandma said sternly. 'The clones are not **toys**. They are only to be used in **emergencies.**'

'OK, got it. Only in emergencies,' said Kenny.

'How do the clones work, Grandma?' I asked.

'You control them using this **headset**,' Grandma said. 'The flip-screen lets you see exactly what your clone is seeing. You give the clone **instructions** by speaking into the **microphone**. Watch. *Nelson, eat your breakfast.*'

My clone immediately started eating my breakfast!

'Impressive!' I said.

'You ain't seen nothing yet!' Grandma said. '*Nelson, eat your breakfast while balancing Kenny's breakfast on your head!*'

'That is the BEST!' I said.

'And he didn't **spill** any of my breakfast, which is the most important thing,' Kenny said.

'Grandma has programmed these robots with every **human action**,' Mum said.

'They're also connected to the **internet,**' Grandma said, 'so they can learn anything new **instantly**. Have a go, boys!'

Coooooool!

'Eat my brussels sprouts, please, Robot Kenny!' Kenny said to his clone. 'While **breakdancing!**'

'You have a go, Nelson,' Grandma said.

'OK,' I said. '*Robot Nelson, please clean the whole kitchen!*'

'*Help him out, Robot Kenny!*' Kenny said to his clone.

Usually, when Kenny and I clean the kitchen it takes us ages because we make up **games**.

But our clones didn't play games. They cleaned up like they had invisible **rockets** on their backs!

They were soooo quick! TOO quick. They both tried to clean the stove at the same time and . . . **BANG!**

The **crash** caused something to pop out of their necks . . . and then the clones started going **NUTS!**

Robot Kenny jumped up on the fridge and started **spinning** on his head.

Robot Nelson danced the **conga line** around the dining room. **By himself!**

'Wow, they really love dancing!' said Kenny.

The robots **knocked over** the table, the chairs and a vase full of flowers.

'We have to stop them before they damage themselves,' Grandma said.

'And **destroy** our living room!' Mum said.

Kenny and I tried to stop the clones but we couldn't catch them!

'Nelson, use your **lasso!**' Mum said.

I grabbed my lasso and **hurled** it at my clone's legs. But he jumped over it like it was a skipping rope!

LEAP!

I called out to Kenny to help me, but when I looked around I saw that he'd stopped helping . . . to have a snack!

But it ended up being the **perfect decoy!** Robot Kenny stopped dancing and came over to **share** Kenny's snack. Grandma quickly put the microchip back into his neck.

Then she reached into Robot Kenny's hair and turned him **off**.

This distracted Robot Nelson long enough for me to **lasso** him.

Grandma put the microchip back in Robot Nelson's neck and turned him off, too. Then she pressed a **button** on each of the headsets and the robots **folded** themselves into **briefcases!**

'You boys are **in charge** of the clones now,' Grandma said. 'Remember, **no-one** can ever find out about them.'

'And they're only to be used in an **emergency**,' Mum reminded us.

THREE

The robot clones made Kenny and I forget all about the **maths test** . . . until it was time to go to school. As we got ready to leave, my nerves hit me like a ton of bricks.

'This is going to be my **worst** test score ever!' I said.

'I bet Sarah will blitz the test. She eats calculations for breakfast!'

'You know who else would **blitz** the test?' Kenny said. 'Our **ROBOT CLONES!**'

'Mum and Grandma said they're only to be used in **emergencies**,' I said.

'We're about to FAIL a maths test, Nelson,' Kenny said. 'This IS an **emergency!**'

‘We can’t use the clones for a maths test,’ I said. ‘It doesn’t **add** up!’

‘Don’t be so **negative!**’ Kenny said.

We shouldn’t be divided on this!

There’s a fraction too much friction!

I wish we got marks for our really bad maths **puns!**

'Grandma designed the clones so people will actually think they're us,' Kenny said. 'Letting them sit the maths test for us is the perfect way to try them out.'

'I suppose it would be good to try,' I said. 'Let's see what Grandma thinks.'

'Grandma's busy inventing a `house-umbrella`,' Kenny said. 'We can't get in.'

'OK, fine,' I said. 'We'll take the clones and decide what to do on the way.'

When we arrived at school, we still hadn't agreed on whether the robot clones should sit the maths test for us.

Everyone in our class was talking about the test, too. As usual, Charles Brock was **bragging**.

My dad says I'm better at maths than Einstein was at my age!

When Charles wasn't bragging, he was **bullying**.

'What's with the briefcases, losers?' Charles said to Kenny and me. 'Are they hiring new workers at the nerd factory?'

'The briefcases contain something **TOP SECRET**,' Kenny said.

Did I mention that Kenny was TERRIBLE at keeping secrets!

'Top secret?!' Charles scoffed. 'I'll be the judge of that!'

He **snatched** Kenny's briefcase out of his hand.

Luckily, Charles couldn't work out how to open it!

Then the bell **rang**. Charles threw Kenny's briefcase to the ground. 'Keep your toy briefcases!' he said. 'You might be nerds, but I am still going to **smash** you both in this test!'

'It's not a competition,' I said.

'It's **always** a competition,' Charles replied. 'And I **always** WIN.'

He turned and strutted into the classroom as if he owned it!

‘Don’t worry about Charles,’ Tiffany said as she walked past.

‘Yeah, he’s just jealous,’ Sarah said. ‘You’re both really smart. You’ll nail the maths test.’

‘Kenny, you were right,’ I said.

‘Great!’ said Kenny. ‘I knew it!’ He paused. ‘About what?’

'This maths test **IS** the perfect time to **try out** our new friends,' I said.

'Nelson agrees with Kenny equals **AWESOME!**' Kenny said. 'But we better get them out quick, the test is about to start!'

We hurried outside the classroom, hid in the bushes, and popped open the briefcases.

The clones **sprang** back to **life**.

'Hi, Robot Kenny!' Kenny said. 'You look more **handsome** than ever!'

'Ready to take a maths test, Robot Nelson?' I asked.

'Can't wait!' Robot Nelson said. 'I LOVE maths tests!'

'Go, go, go!' Kenny said to the clones.

'Wait, wait, wait!' I said. 'Don't answer

ALL the questions correctly, or Mr Fletcher will get **suspicious.**'

'We're smart, but not that smart!' Kenny said.

'We'll get 81 per cent,' Robot Nelson said.

'You can't both get 81 per cent, or it will look like we copied each other!' I said.

'I'll get 79 per cent,' said Robot Kenny.

'Hey! Why do I get the lower score?!' Kenny asked.

'No time to argue,' I said, 'the test is about to start!'

'Fine,' Kenny said. 'But next spelling test, **my** clone gets the top score!'

'Next test?! Kenny, this is the first and last test the clones take for us,' I said. Then I turned to the clones. 'After the test, make sure you hurry back here and swap back with us.'

'Will do!' Robot Kenny and Robot Nelson said at the same time.

We watched through our **headsets** as our robot clones ran into the classroom and quietly sat in our seats. Sarah looked across and gave my clone a thumbs up.

Robot Nelson just **stared** at her.

'Give her a thumbs up back!' I said to my clone through the microphone.

Then Robot Nelson put his thumb up his nose!

'Not like THAT!' I said to my clone. 'Forget it, just focus on the test. Good luck!'

As Kenny and I waited for our clones to finish the test, we lay down and had a nice rest.

FOUR

We were woken up by our clones rushing back out to us.

'How did you go?' I asked nervously.

'81 per cent!' Robot Nelson said.

'79 per cent!' Robot Kenny said.

'Great job, guys!' Kenny said.

'Did anyone suspect you weren't the real Nelson and Kenny?' I asked.

'What do you mean?' Robot Kenny asked.

'We *are* the real Nelson and Kenny!' Robot Nelson said.

Then they both laughed.

'Time to get back in your briefcases, guys!' I said.

'Not yet,' Kenny said. 'They need to do more than quietly sit a maths test to trick Dr Kane. He's a **CRIMINAL MASTERMIND**.'

'Good point,' I said. 'What are you thinking?'

'Let's see if they can convince Sarah and Tiffany they're the real Nelson and Kenny.'

‘That’s a very **bad** idea,’ I said.

‘It’s a brilliant idea!’ Kenny said. ‘And besides, this is not just about me and you, Nelson, it’s about saving Duck Creek!’

‘Guys,’ I said to the clones. ‘We need you to talk to Sarah and Tiffany and convince them you’re us.’

‘It’s what we were made to do!’ said Robot Nelson.

'Actually,' Kenny said, 'can you act like us, but be a tiny bit more . . . *charming?*'

'Kenny, I thought we were doing this to save Duck Creek?!'

'We are. Doesn't mean we can't have **fun!**'

'How much more charming do you want us to be?' Robot Kenny asked.

'33 per cent more should do it!' Kenny said.

The clones nodded and **strolled** over to Tiffany and Sarah.

'Hi, Sarah and Tiffany,' Robot Nelson said. 'Lovely day for the **race.**'

'What race?' Tiffany asked.

'The **Human Race.**' Robot Kenny said.

Sarah and Tiffany chuckled.

That's terrible!
It's not even 10 per
cent more charming!

Shhh . . .
at least they
laughed!

'You guys did brilliantly on the maths test,' Sarah said.

'Not as well as you two,' Robot Nelson said.

'What's it like being smart and cool?' Robot Kenny asked.

'Wow! You've both taken your *charming* pills this morning!' Tiffany said.

'Guys, can you answer a question we've been meaning to ask you for ages?' Sarah said.

'Of course!' Robot Nelson said.

'You can ask us anything you like,' Robot Kenny said.

'How come every time Ninja Kid and H-Dude appear, you both go missing?' Tiffany asked.

Kenny and I looked at each other nervously.

'Ahhhhh . . .' I said into my microphone.

'Ummm . . .' Kenny said into his.

'Be honest,' Tiffany said. 'Are **you** . . . Ninja Kid and H-Dude?'

Unless we came up with something quick, our identities were about to be **revealed!**

Kenny and I both grabbed our emergency backpacks . . .

and then Ninja Kid and H-Dude **BURST** onto the playground!

'Hi, Tiffany. Hi, Sarah,' Kenny said.

'We were just talking about you two!' Sarah said.

'What are you doing here?' Tiffany asked.

'We're just making sure you haven't had any more **trouble** from **Dr Kane,'** I said.

'We haven't seen Dr Kane since last time we saw you,' Sarah said.

'Glad to hear it!' Kenny said. 'Oh, and who are your smart, funny, very good-looking friends?' he added, pointing to our clones.

'I'm Kenny,' Robot Kenny said.

'I'm Nelson,' Robot Nelson said.

'We're Ninja Kid and H-Dude. Nice to meet you guys,' I said.

'You definitely look like the **COOLEST** boys in the school!' Kenny said. He was really enjoying this!

I was too - it was strange being Ninja Kid and H-Dude and not having a crisis to deal with!

'Well, we're glad Dr Kane hasn't returned,' I said.

'Keep doing what you're doing! See ya!' Kenny said.

Then we **Flew OFF** on our jetpacks.

When lunchtime was over, the clones came back to the bushes and we put them away in their briefcases. Then we walked into class as if it was any other day.

FiVE

The next morning was the day of **SCHOOL CAMP**.

Kenny and I gave Mum and Grandma a kiss and a hug goodbye. Then we tried to rush off.

'Hang on!' Grandma said.

'Why do we have to take the clones to camp?' I asked.

'A school camp is just the sort of place Dr Kane might target,' Grandma said. 'You need to be prepared.'

On the bus, Kenny and I weren't our usual chatty selves.

We still felt really **BAD** about **lying** to Mum and Grandma.

'Why are you two so **gloomy?**' Sarah said, leaning over our seats.

'Aren't you **pumped** about Camp Koala?' Tiffany asked.

'Yeah. We're really **excited**,' I said, trying to fake it.

'We are so excited it's making us quiet,' Kenny said.

'So how was it finally meeting Ninja Kid and H-Dude?' Tiffany asked.

'It was fine,' I said.

'They didn't really do much,' Kenny said, trying not to smile.

'They were checking to make sure we're OK,' Sarah said. 'I think that was a *lovely* thing to do.'

'H-Dude is the best,' Tiffany said.

Kenny didn't know whether he should feel **happy** or **jealous!**

All the kids **CHEERED** when we finally arrived at Camp Koala!

It was a beautiful campsite, nestled in amongst trees as **BIG** as dinosaurs.

When we got off the bus we were greeted by the camp leader, **Captain Koala**.

Welcome to Camp Koala!

He spoke through a megaphone even though we were only standing a few metres away from him!

'I'd like to introduce you to my two assistants. Firstly, this is **Ruff!**'

A funny-looking **dog** bounded up to Captain Koala.

'Say hi to the kids, Ruff,' Captain Koala said.

'**Ruff!**' barked Ruff.

All the kids **laughed**. But the little dog didn't seem to think it was very funny . . .

'I'd also like to introduce **Bonsai!**' Captain Koala said. A **man dressed like a tree** stepped out from the bushes!

Bonsai **waved** but didn't speak.

'This place is **NUTSO!**' Kenny whispered.

'Camp Koala will **challenge** you like you've never been challenged before,' Captain Koala said.

'I can handle it,' Charles bragged, looking at Tiffany. 'I've been camping since before you were born!'

'Well,' said Tiffany. '**I've** been going camping since **before** I was born!'

'Don't be ridiculous, that's not even possible!' scoffed Charles.

'Yes it is. My mum went camping when I was in her tummy!' Tiffany said.

'It's time for your first challenge,' Captain Koala said. 'The first two teams to set up their tents get their choice of **dessert** tonight!'

'Double choc-chip, caramel ice-cream with chocolate topping!' Kenny called out.

'Hang on, Kenny!' I said. 'We haven't even started the challenge yet!'

'I've never wanted to **win** so much in my life!' Kenny said. 'Let's get this tent up!'

All the other kids **rushed** to put their tents up. But it didn't take us long to realise that **rushing** and tents just don't go together!

Everyone was making **mistakes**. Sarah and Tiffany put their tent up **back to front!**

Billy Bob and Evan set up their tent on a huge **pile of rocks!**

And Kenny and I pitched our tent **upside down!**

'This is a **disaster!**' I said. 'We've got no chance of winning now.'

'Unless . . .' Kenny said. 'We give our clones a little more **practice!**'

'I don't know, Kenny,' I said. 'Grandma and Mum said only in emergencies . . .'

Then Charles called out, 'Turn that frown **upside down**, losers! And while you're at it, turn your tent the right way up!'

'Alright!' I said to Kenny. 'We'll call in the clones. But this is the **last time** we use them for anything other than beating Dr Kane.'

'**Yesss!**' Kenny said.

We snuck into the bushes, opened our briefcases and set our clones **free!**

'Robot Kenny and Robot Nelson, we need you to put up a tent,' I said.

'Faster than anyone's ever pitched a tent before!' Kenny added.

Before we could even blink, Robot Kenny and Robot Nelson had set up our tent! They worked so fast it was like a mini cyclone. **A clone cyclone!**

'Wow!' said Kenny. 'That was **in-tents!**'

'We have a **winner!**' Captain Koala said.

As Charles was staring at our tent in shock, he **tripped** over his own tent and knocked it over.

Tiffany and Sarah turned their tent the right way around and came **second**.

'Congratulations, Nelson, Kenny, Sarah and Tiffany,' Captain Koala said. 'You've won the first challenge and your choice of dessert tonight!'

'Whatever you guys said to each other in the bushes really worked!' Sarah said to our clones.

'Yeah, you were like two **totally different kids** after that!' Tiffany said.

'Act cool, guys!' I said into my microphone.

'And don't forget *charming*!' added Kenny.

'We were **FASTER**, but you were more *stylish*,' said Robot Kenny.

'Winning is even better when we get to share it with you,' said Robot Nelson.

The girls smiled.

SiX

We were about to call our clones back when Captain Koala announced,

'The tent challenge was easy compared to your next task - the CRAZY CANOEING COURSE!'

'We should swap back with the clones,' I whispered to Kenny.

'Let's wait till we get to the river and there are more distractions,' Kenny said.

'Good plan!' I said.

We stayed out of sight as we followed everyone down to the river.

The river had the **biggest** white water rapids I had ever seen!

'Maybe we should give the clones one final test!' Kenny said.

'C'mon, Kenny, they've already convinced everyone they're us.'

'This course is **HARD**, Nelson! If we do this, we could look like losers and ruin everything.'

I glanced over at Tiffany and Sarah. They were whispering to each other and smiling at our clones.

'Fine,' I said. 'But this is **positively, absolutely, definitely,** the last time we use them unless it's a real emergency!'

Kenny and I watched as everyone got into their canoes. Captain Koala counted down to the start of the race.

'Let's wait at the finish line so we can swap with the clones straight after the race,' I said.

'Good thinking!' Kenny said.

We stayed out of sight as we ran behind trees, rocks and shrubs to the finish line. We found a great hiding spot in the **hollow** of a large tree!

From there, we watched through our headsets to see how the canoe race was going.

Charles got off to a really quick start. So did Billy Bob, Sarah and Tiffany. Our clones were in the middle of the pack but they were getting better at canoeing by the second!

As Robot Kenny caught up to Tiffany, Kenny **whispered** into his microphone, 'Robot Kenny, wave at Tiffany and say something charming!'

Our clones were paddling **super quickly** now. They passed Billy Bob.

When they passed Charles, he wasn't quite so encouraging.

Kenny whispered into his microphone. 'Robot Kenny, splash Charles!'

Charles was seriously **cranky**. But there wasn't much he could do about it. Our clones were already **WAAAAY AHEAD.**

'Great work, you two!' Captain Koala shouted through his megaphone.

'We can't let them go too fast. Let's have both our robots tie for first place, Kenny,' I said to him.

But Kenny was already whispering something into his microphone. When I looked back at my flip-screen I saw that Robot Kenny was **streaking ahead** of my clone at ***LIGHTNING SPEED!***

'What are you doing?!' I asked Kenny.

'Testing how quick he can go!'

Kenny said. 'Wow, he's faster than a speedboat!'

Robot Nelson was catching up, paddling super fast too. The two clones were **neck and neck** as they raced down the **final** rapids.

There wasn't even a **whisker** between our two clones as they approached the finish line.

But we'd pushed our clones **TOO FAR**. Suddenly, they started paddling in **circles**.

They looked like two mini **tornadoes!**

WHOA!

WHOA!

The clones were **spinning** around and around. Faster and faster until . . .

With their microchips loose again, they immediately stopped caring about the race. Both robot clones **jumped up** and started **dancing** in their canoes!

'Less dancing, more rowing!' I said to my clone through the microphone.

'You can dance once you've won!' Kenny said to his clone.

But it was no use. The clones couldn't take instructions. Robot Kenny jumped into Robot Nelson's canoe and they started **dancing together!**

'I knew I'd catch you in the end! **Booyah!**' Charles said as he raced past the clones and . . .

. . . WON the race!

Next, Tiffany and Sarah paddled past. 'Interesting moves, you two!' Sarah said, smiling.

'Kenny, we have to stop them before everyone realises they're **clones**,' I said.

'How can we stop them?' Kenny asked. 'They're **faster** than us. They're smarter than us. And they're much better **DANCERS** than us!'

'I've got an **idea,**' I said.

I jumped down and quickly made a lasso out of some tree vines.

As our classmates were busy getting their place numbers, I tried to **lasso** Robot Kenny and Robot Nelson . . .

but Robot Nelson dipped Robot Kenny and the lasso went right over the top of them.

SWOOSH!

'Great work, campers!' Captain Koala said to the class. 'Now leave your canoes by the riverbank and let's walk to the camp hall.'

Robot Nelson joined Robot Kenny's **CONGA LINE**, and the rest of the class followed!

‘We’ll never be able to **switch back** with them now,’ I said.

‘I’m sorry, Nelson, I shouldn’t have tried to win the race,’ Kenny said. ‘It’s just . . . I wanted to be the **STAR** for once.’

‘You are a star, Kenny. You’ve never lost an eating competition, you’re super funny and you’re the best friend and cousin in the world.’

‘Oh, shucks,’ Kenny said. ‘Let’s hug it out.’

'Whoa!' I said.

'Yeah, it was a good hug!' Kenny said.

'No, look! Your clone has **broken away!** You hide while I **distract** him,' I said. 'Then race over and turn him off.'

'How will you distract him?' Kenny asked.

'By doing the **ROBOT DANCE** of course!' I said.

It worked! Robot Kenny hurried over to me and started doing the **ROBOT DANCE**, too!

The real Kenny rushed over to us. But just as he was about to turn his clone off, Robot Kenny did a **backflip** and escaped the real Kenny's grasp!

FLIP!

Kenny chased after his clone and **TACKLED** him to the ground!

As they **wrestled** on the grass, I grabbed my vine **lasso**. But I didn't know which one to capture!

'Which of you is the real Kenny?' I asked.

They **flipped** and **turned** each other on the grass.

'What are you waiting for, Nelson?' one Kenny said. 'Lasso my clone!'

'He's trying to **trick** you, Nelson,' the other Kenny said. 'He's the clone!'

I was so confused. They looked and sounded exactly the same! Then one of the Kennys stopped wrestling and started eating **popcorn!**

Only the **real Kenny** would eat at such an inappropriate time! I quickly lassoed the other Kenny, pinning his arms to his waist.

The real Kenny reached into the clone's hair and turned him **OFF**. Robot Kenny became lifeless and **floppy**.

Kenny pushed the microchip back into his neck and folded him into his briefcase.

'Great work, Kenny!' I said.

'Thanks, Nelson. But what about your clone? He's probably running wild in the camp hall.'

'You head in there and put the microchip back in his neck,' I said. 'Then I can control him again.'

'Sounds like a plan!' Kenny said. 'Wish me luck!'

SEVEN

I waited outside the camp hall as Kenny rushed inside with his briefcase. All of a sudden the hall door **SLAMMED** shut and the **shutters** came down. It was **locked!**

I couldn't see a thing . . . until my **headset** came back to life. Kenny must have found Robot Nelson and put the microchip back in!

I could see that Kenny and the rest of the class were gathered in front of a

HARDCORE OBSTACLE COURSE!

Captain Koala was standing on top of a ***warped wall***. Ruff and Bonsai were either side of him.

Kenny had his hand up. 'When do we get our special desserts?' he asked.

'You might not be hungry after this,' Captain Koala said.

'You've obviously never met Kenny!' Tiffany said.

Everyone **laughed**, except Captain Koala and his assistants.

'Before you begin the obstacle course, there's something you should know,' Captain Koala said. The kids were all listening intently. 'I'm not really **Captain Koala . . .**'

IT WAS DR KANE!

As well as wearing his disguise, he had been using a special device to **change his voice**. But now he'd turned it off and he sounded as **EVIL** as ever.

I felt **useless**. I couldn't do anything to help when I was locked outside!

'Did you really believe I was a human-sized koala?!' Dr Kane laughed. 'I suppose you thought my assistants were a dog and a tree, too!'

Then Ruff the dog took off his disguise . . .

It was Dr Kane's evil **chipmunk** sidekick,

EINSTEIN!

Just when things couldn't get any stranger, the tree busted out of its costume to reveal . . . a **NINJA!**

'Meet the greatest ninja alive,' Dr Kane said. 'I call him **ULTIMATE NINJA!**'

'We have brought your class here for one reason,' Dr Kane said. 'To find **NiNJA KiD.'**

'Don't move a muscle,' I said to my clone through the microphone. Luckily, he was listening to me now.

'Show yourself, Ninja Kid!' Dr Kane shouted to the class.

'I told you Ninja Kid was a **coward**,' Einstein said. 'More like **Whinger Kid** than Ninja Kid . . . "Ooooh, I'm too much of a **scaredy cat** to show my face."'

'I know you're here, Ninja Kid,' Dr Kane continued. 'I have some idea of your true identity after the canoe race, but I will know for sure after I make you all attempt the **world's TOUGHEST obstacle course.**'

'Don't just sit there like bowls of **jelly**,' Dr Kane yelled. 'Form an orderly queue at the start of the obstacle course!'

Through my headset, I could see my class looked frightened as they lined up. Charles looked the most scared. He was **shaking** like a leaf as he hid behind everyone else.

'**Wait!**' Kenny yelled to the kids. 'We don't have to do what he says. He's not our camp leader. He's a **CRIMINAL!**'

'Tell them that Kenny's right,' I said through the microphone to my clone.

'Kenny's right!' Robot Nelson said.

'Kenny and Nelson are right!' Sarah said.

'Kenny, Nelson and Sarah are right!' Tiffany said.

Gradually, all the kids started stepping out of the queue.

'Fools!' Einstein said.

'Now we have to do this the **hard** way,' Dr Kane said. He pointed to the ninja. 'Show them what you can do!'

Until now, the **ULTIMATE NINJA** had stayed perfectly still. But he suddenly **sprang** to life, leaping high above the rolling bars . . .

Then he did a **triple roundhouse kick** in the air!

Dr Kane threw a **watermelon** at the **ULTIMATE NINJA** and he sliced it into pieces . . . with his hands! While he was still in the air!

Then the **ULTIMATE NINJA** landed on the floor as if he was as light as a feather.

'Ninja Kid, I will keep your whole class here until you come forward,' Dr Kane said.

Even if I wanted to show myself, I couldn't. I was trapped outside. This was a **nightmare**.

'You leave me no choice!' Dr Kane said. He nodded at the ninja.

I watched through my headset as the **ULTIMATE NINJA** leapt high into the air again. As he reached the top of his leap, he started **spinning**. His legs were moving so fast, they looked like a **human blender!**

The spinning ninja started moving towards the class. They were about to get sliced and diced!

Suddenly, Kenny sprang forward.

'Halt!' Dr Kane yelled to the **ULTIMATE NINJA**.

The **ULTIMATE NINJA** pulled out of his spinning-blade kick and landed on the floor.

'Haha! I knew we'd smoke him out!' Einstein said to Dr Kane.

Dr Kane pointed at Kenny. 'Get him, **ULTIMATE NINJA!'**

The **ULTIMATE NINJA** climbed up the **glass elevator** and stood looming above Kenny. Just as he was about to jump, Sarah stepped forward.

'No, I'm Ninja Kid!' Tiffany said.

Then **ALL** the kids stood up - they all had socks wrapped around their heads!

I'm Ninja Kid!

I'm Ninja Kid!

I'm Ninja Kid!

I'm Ninja Kid!

I'm Ninja Kid!

'C'mon, I'm definitely Ninja Kid,' Charles Brock said. 'I mean, look at me!'

He'd finally stopped hiding!

'You dare play games with me?!' Dr Kane boomed. He was getting really **ANGRY** now.

I really needed to get inside the hall . . . fast! I looked up and saw a small open window high up.

'You have no idea how powerful my **ULTIMATE NINJA** is!' Dr Kane yelled.

The **ULTIMATE NINJA** took several steps backwards then ran towards the class with **electric speed**. He **LEAPT** and spun like a **human drill**.

I put on my Ninja Kid disguise and flipped through the open window.

I landed right in the path of the **ULTIMATE NINJA'S** spinning!

'Nice of you to finally join us, Ninja Kid!' Dr Kane said. 'Prepare to be defeated!'

EIGHT

As I stood face to face with the **ULTIMATE NINJA**, I knew there was no way I could **beat** him.

Sure I was a ninja, but I was a **NINJA KID**. He was a ninja MAN! A ninja man that could spin like a **drill!**

'You've got this, Ninja Kid,' Kenny said.

'Go, Ninja Kid!' Sarah yelled.

'I miss H-Dude!' Tiffany said.

I didn't have time to soak in the encouragement - the **ULTIMATE NINJA** was **hurling** ninja discs at me!

Luckily, I had lots of practice at this. Grandma was always throwing paint lids at me to keep me on my toes!

I dodged the first, second and third ninja discs. But then the **ULTIMATE NINJA** started throwing two discs at once!

FLiNG! FLiNG!

FLiNG!

It took all my **concentration** and agility to dodge the spinning discs. I was **bobbing** and **weaving** like a clown at a pie throwing contest!

The discs were coming quicker and quicker. They were shooting out of the **ULTIMATE NINJA'S** hands so fast, it seemed like he had eight arms. He was like the **OCTO-NINJA!**

When the **ULTIMATE NINJA** finally ran out of discs, I gathered up the ones near me and threw them back at him.

The **ULTIMATE NINJA** turned and ran up the warped wall, glided across the unstable bridge and climbed the rungless ladder!

I thought I had him **trapped,** but he easily ducked and weaved the ninja discs. He was so fast and agile!

'Think fast, **ULTIMATE NINJA!'** Dr Kane said. He hurled a **ninja staff** at the Ultimate Ninja.

The Ultimate Ninja caught the staff and used it to send the ninja discs flying back at me!

I had to get away . . . and fast! I quickly scanned the hall and decided my best chance was to run through the obstacle course.

I dashed through the **half pipe** and hurried across the flying bars.

Then I **launched** myself into the air with my jetpack. I circled around the hall, behind the Bridge of Blades, and came at the **ULTIMATE NINJA** with Grandma's lasso.

But the **ULTIMATE NINJA** was too quick for me. He did a somersault to dodge the lasso and flung the staff straight at me.

The ninja staff **SPEARED** through my jetpack, sending me Spiralling out of control!

I **fell** to the floor . . .

CRASSHHHH!

CRACK!

and **broke** my jetpack!

'Disappointing, Ninja Kid!' Dr Kane said. 'I thought you'd put up more of a fight!'

'Yeah!' said Einstein. 'Ninja Kid? More like **Injure Kid!**'

'Finish him!' said Dr Kane.

The **ULTIMATE NINJA** nodded, jumped in the air and **spiralled** towards me!

The kids all **gasped** as the **ULTIMATE NINJA** came **flying** towards me like a human corkscrew. He was so **fast**, there was nothing I could do. Until, suddenly something knocked him right out of mid-air!

OOSH!

While everyone was distracted by my **battle** with the Ultimate Ninja, Kenny had released his clone from the briefcase and put on his H-Dude disguise.

The kids **cheered** and **clapped**. Tiffany was really **excited**!

This was **AWESOME**. I was so proud of Kenny. 'I told you that you were a **STAR!**' I called to him.

'Thanks, Ninja Kid!' Kenny called back.

With H-Dude by my side, I had more **courage** to face the Ultimate Ninja.

I looked him right in the eyes . . .

I expected to see pure hate staring back, but I saw almost the **opposite**. I had the strangest feeling I'd seen those eyes before. But I couldn't imagine where. It's not like you see ninjas every day in the supermarket!

Apart from looking in the mirror, this was the first time **I'd** even met another **ninja!**

The **ULTIMATE NINJA** was getting ready to strike. '**I**'m sorry,' he said, 'but **I** must obey my order.'

He bowed, and that's when **I** saw it . . .

A microchip! Exactly like the robot clones!

'H-Dude, look!' I whispered to Kenny, pointing at the microchip.

Kenny nodded. 'I've got a plan!'

'Tie him up!' Dr Kane said and threw the **ULTIMATE NINJA** a rope.

The Ultimate Ninja did a triple flip and was about to tie me up when . . . Kenny started doing the **ROBOT DANCE!**

It was a pretty **strange** plan . . . but it **worked!** The Ultimate Ninja was only distracted for a split second, but it was long enough for me to pluck the **microchip** out.

I was ready for the **ULTIMATE NINJA** to start **GOING NUTS** like the clones did when they lost their microchips. But he didn't. He just fell **asleep!**

When I looked closely at the Ultimate Ninja, I realised he was not a **ROBOT** like our clones. He was **human!** I had that feeling again . . .

Suddenly, Dr Kane **pushed** me away. He grabbed the Ultimate Ninja's shoulders. 'Get up!' he yelled.

Einstein joined him. 'Yeah, this is no time for a nap!'

But they couldn't wake him.

'What have you done?' shouted Dr Kane. He took something out of his pocket and threw it on the floor.

It was a **SMOKE BOMB!**

We couldn't see a thing. Commotion erupted inside the hall. Kenny and I fought our way through the haze just in time to see Dr Kane carrying the **ULTIMATE NINJA** outside.

We **rushed** after them but by the time we got outside, Dr Kane, Einstein and the sleeping ninja were **flying away** in Kane's **helicopter**.

Everyone was so happy that we had saved the day once more.

'Go, Ninja Kid!' Sarah said.

'Amazing work, H-Dude!' Tiffany said.

We even made our clones congratulate us too!

'Thanks for all your **encouragement!**' I said.

'Yeah, we couldn't have done it without you!' Kenny said.

'Hey, Nelson and Kenny, can you walk us out of the campsite?' I said to our clones.

The rest of the class **waved goodbye**.

Once we were away from the other kids, Kenny and I got changed and said goodbye to our clones.

'You did a brilliant job, guys,' I said.

'No-one will guess our **true identities** now,' Kenny said.

'See you soon!' Robot Nelson said.

'I liked being you!' Robot Kenny said.

Putting the clones back in their briefcases was a little **emotional!**

When we returned to the camp hall, Sarah and Tiffany **rushed** over to us.

'I can't believe you guys got to walk out Ninja Kid and H-Dude!' Sarah said.

'H-Dude is soooo cool!' Tiffany added.

'Yeah, he's alright!' Kenny said, *blushing*.

NiNE

When we arrived home from camp, we told Mum and Grandma **EVERYTHING.**

They were **relieved** we had managed to stop another attack from Dr Kane. But they were **really disappointed** when we told them we'd let our clones take the maths test, and compete in the tent competition and the canoe race.

'You made things a lot more **dangerous** by not listening to us,' Grandma said. 'I need to know that when I ask you to do something, you can both be trusted.'

'It was all my fault,' Kenny said. 'I got carried away with this **perfect** new version of myself.'

'I did, too,' I said.

'Well, you know there will have to be **CONSEQUENCES**,' Mum said sternly.

'Oh man,' Kenny said. 'Consequences are never good.'

'I'm going to take back the clones,' Grandma said. 'They've served their purpose and I'm not sure you can be trusted with them until you're older.'

Kenny and I both nodded sadly.

I miss them already!

'And you'll both have to re-sit the maths test,' Mum said.

NOOOOO!

'This time try actually **studying** for the test,' Grandma suggested.

Instead of having eating competitions or practising your lasso!

We were just about to eat dinner when I remembered something. 'There was something strange about the **ULTIMATE NINJA,'** I said to Grandma and Mum. 'I think I . . . recognised him.'

'What did he look like?' Mum asked.

'He wore a ninja suit that covered everything but his eyes,' I said. 'But I did get this!'

Grandma studied the microchip carefully. 'This looks very familiar,' she said.

'What does it do?' Kenny asked.

'It can be used to **control the mind** of another being,' Grandma said.

'It was one of the inventions Dr Kane stole from me when he ran away.'

'Nelson,' Grandma said with her most serious voice, 'I think the Ultimate Ninja is **YOUR FATHER.**'

'No way!' I said. 'Why would my own dad want to fight me?'

'Because he wasn't thinking for himself,' Mum said. 'His thoughts are being **controlled** by Dr Kane.'

'Dr Kane has inserted something very special into this microchip,' Grandma said.

'A purple diamond!' Kenny exclaimed.

'A **hypno** diamond,' Grandma corrected. 'I've been doing some research. You need to crush many purple stones to make just one of these. And the stones are incredibly rare. Duck Creek may be the only place in the world where they are found.'

'That's why Dr Kane wants everyone to leave?' I asked.

'Exactly,' Mum said. 'So he can mine the entire town.'

'Too much **doom and gloom!'** Kenny said. 'Apple crumble time?!'

'OK,' Mum laughed.

'Yessss!' Kenny said.

'Will Dad be OK?' I asked.

'I don't think Dr Kane would ever hurt his twin brother,' Mum said.

'But he'll probably have another microchip,' Grandma said sadly. 'Then your dad will be **under his control** once more.'

'I hate the idea that he's being made to do things he would never do,' Mum said.

'I promise, Mum, Kenny and I will bring Dad home one day.'

Mum smiled. 'I know you will.'

READ THEM ALL!

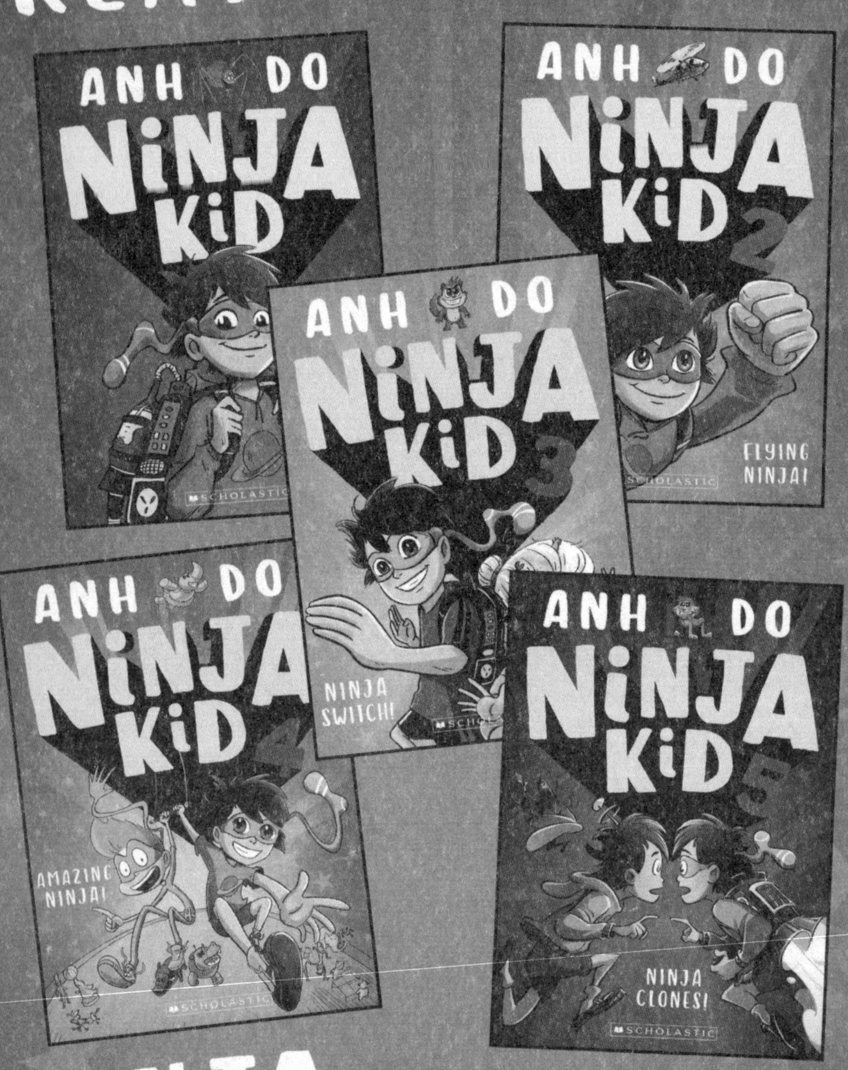

NINJA KID 6 COMING SOON!